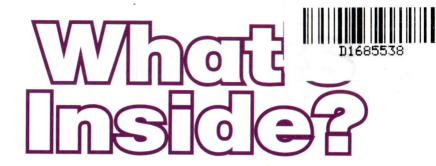

What's Inside?

Written by Monica Hughes

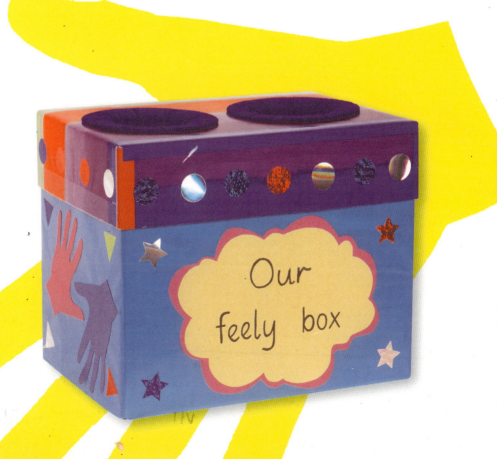

Our feely box

What's inside?

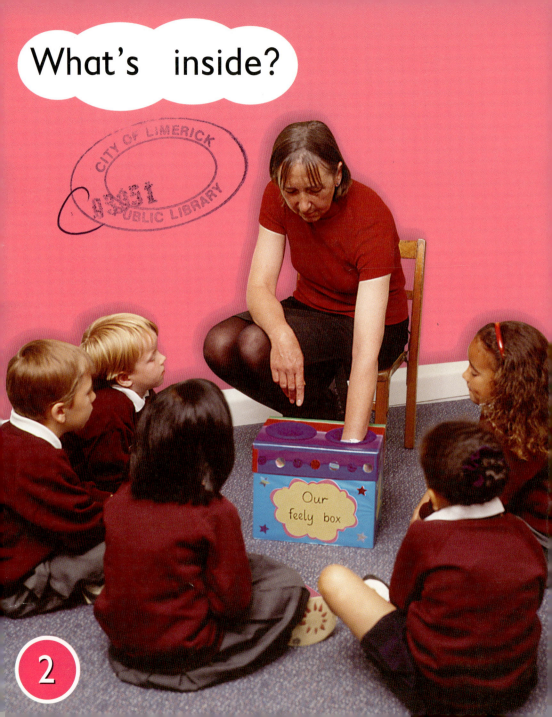

Our feely box

2

It is hard.

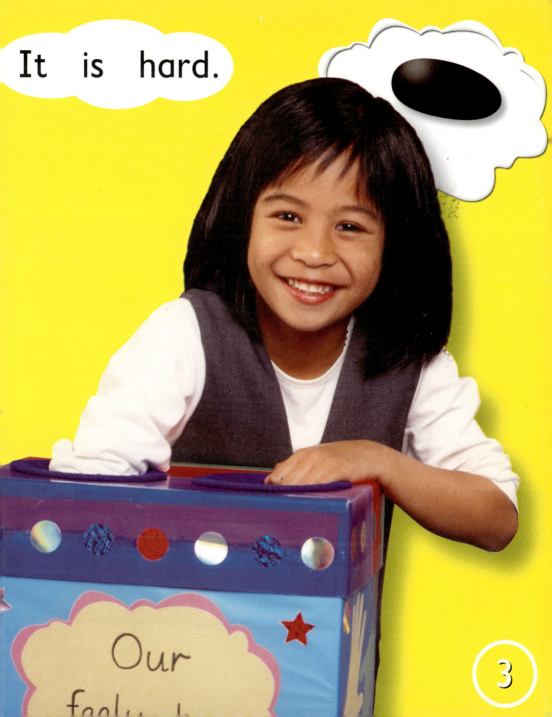

3

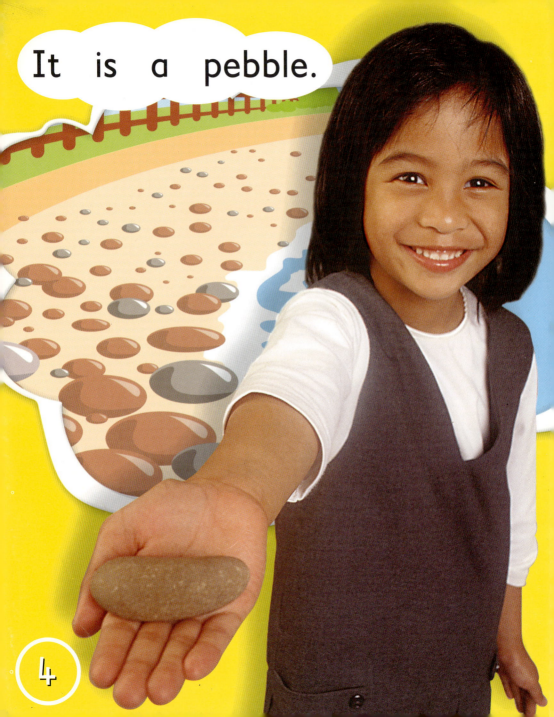

It is a pebble.

4

It is round.

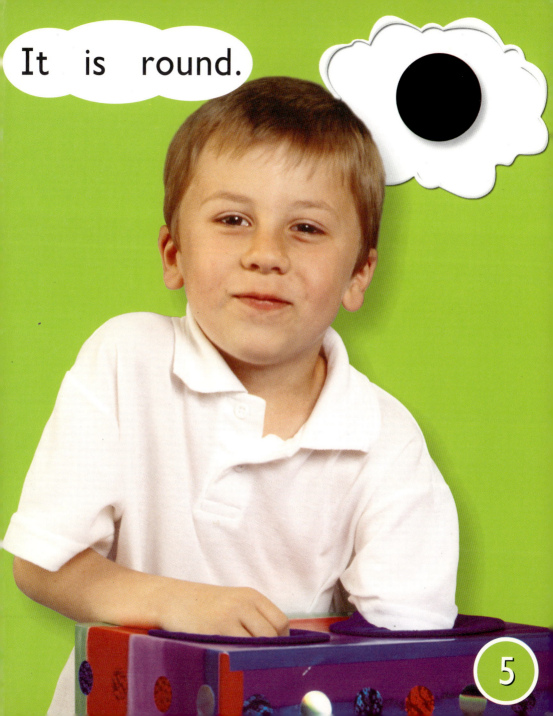

It is a ball.

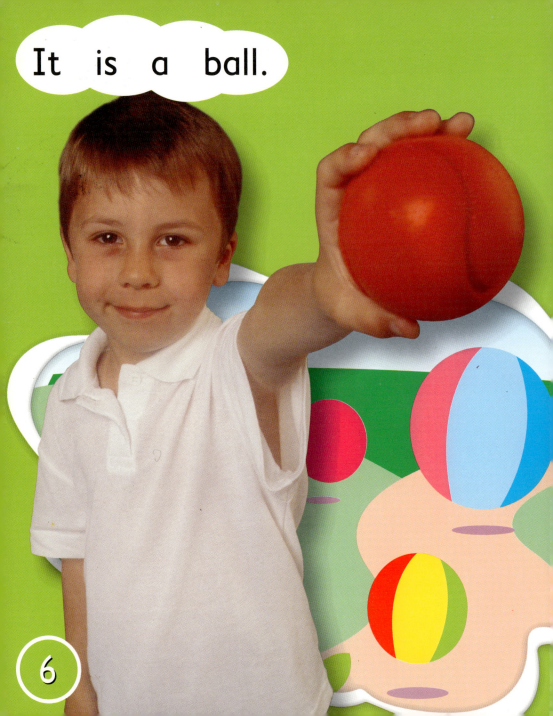

6

It is bumpy.

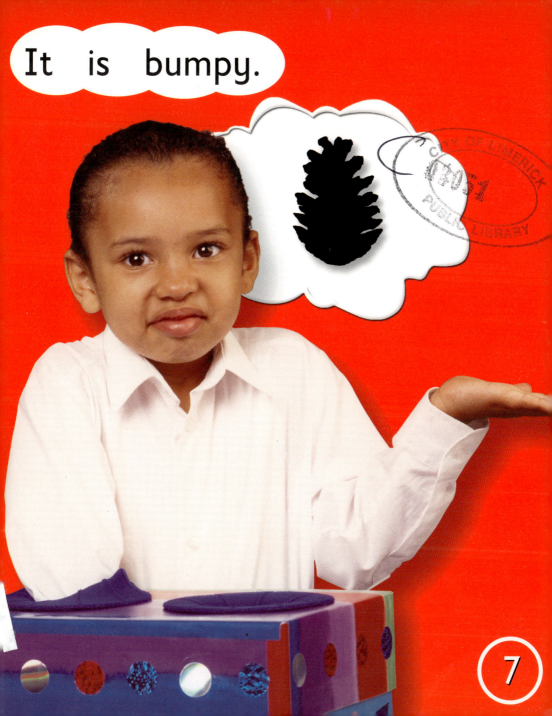

7

It is a cone.

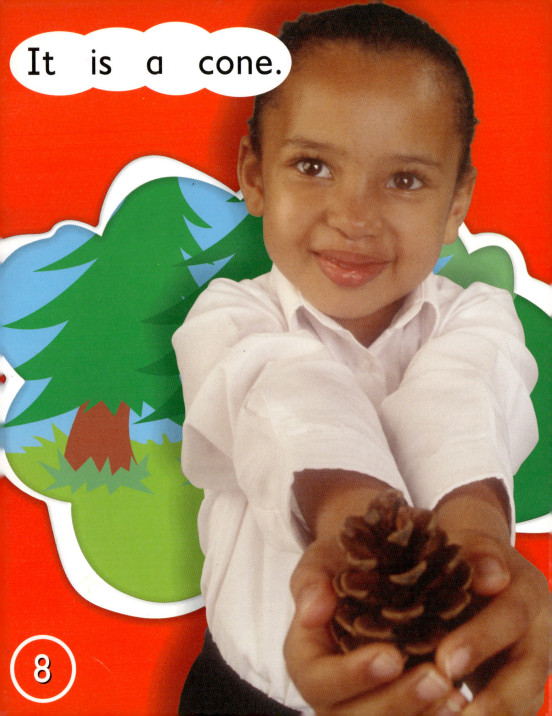

8

It is silky.

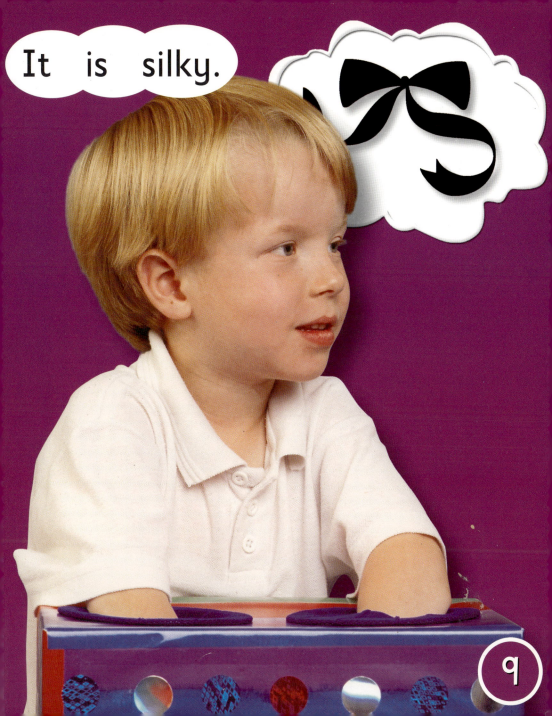

9

It is a ribbon.

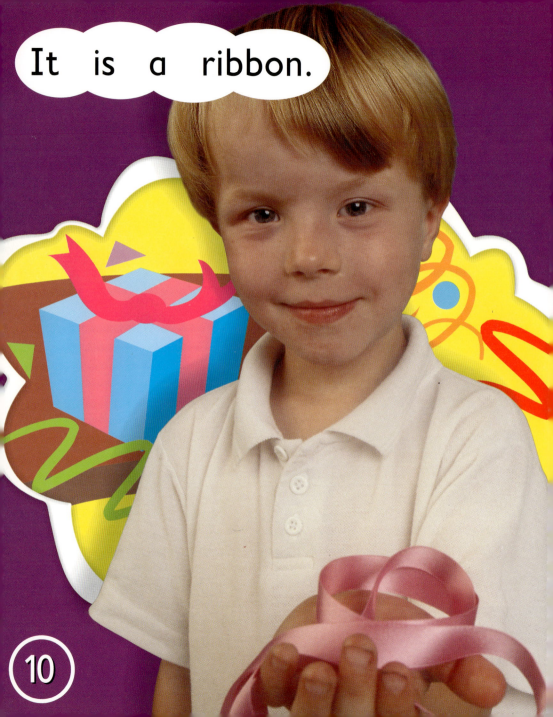

10

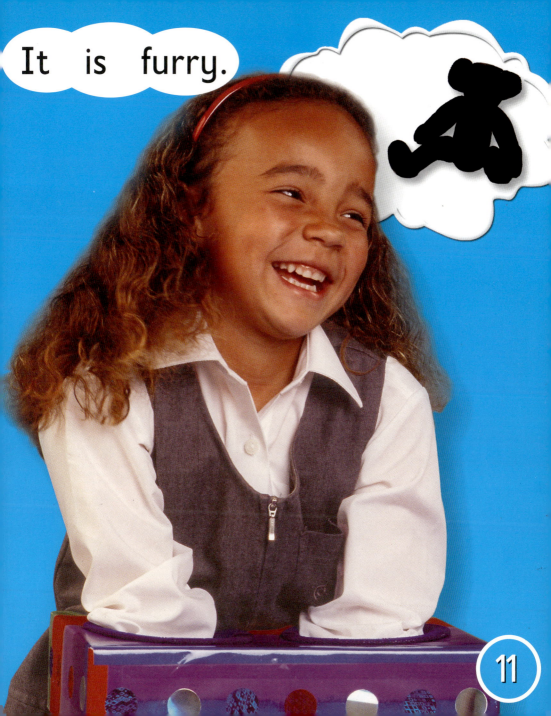

It is furry.

11

It is a teddy!

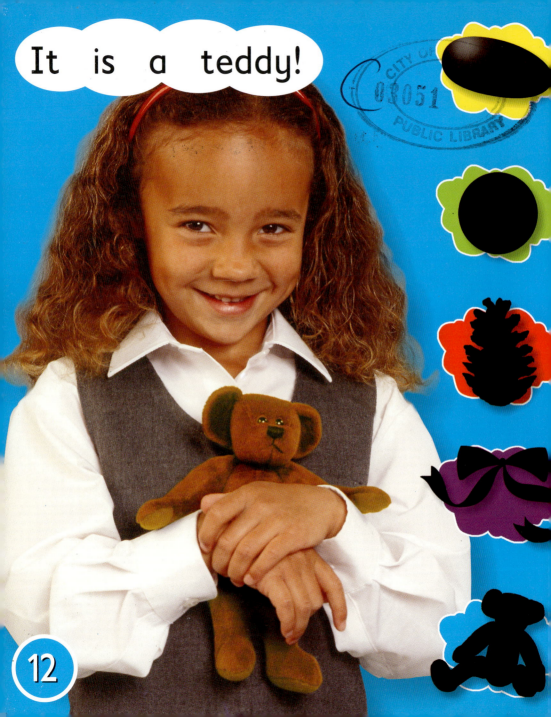

12